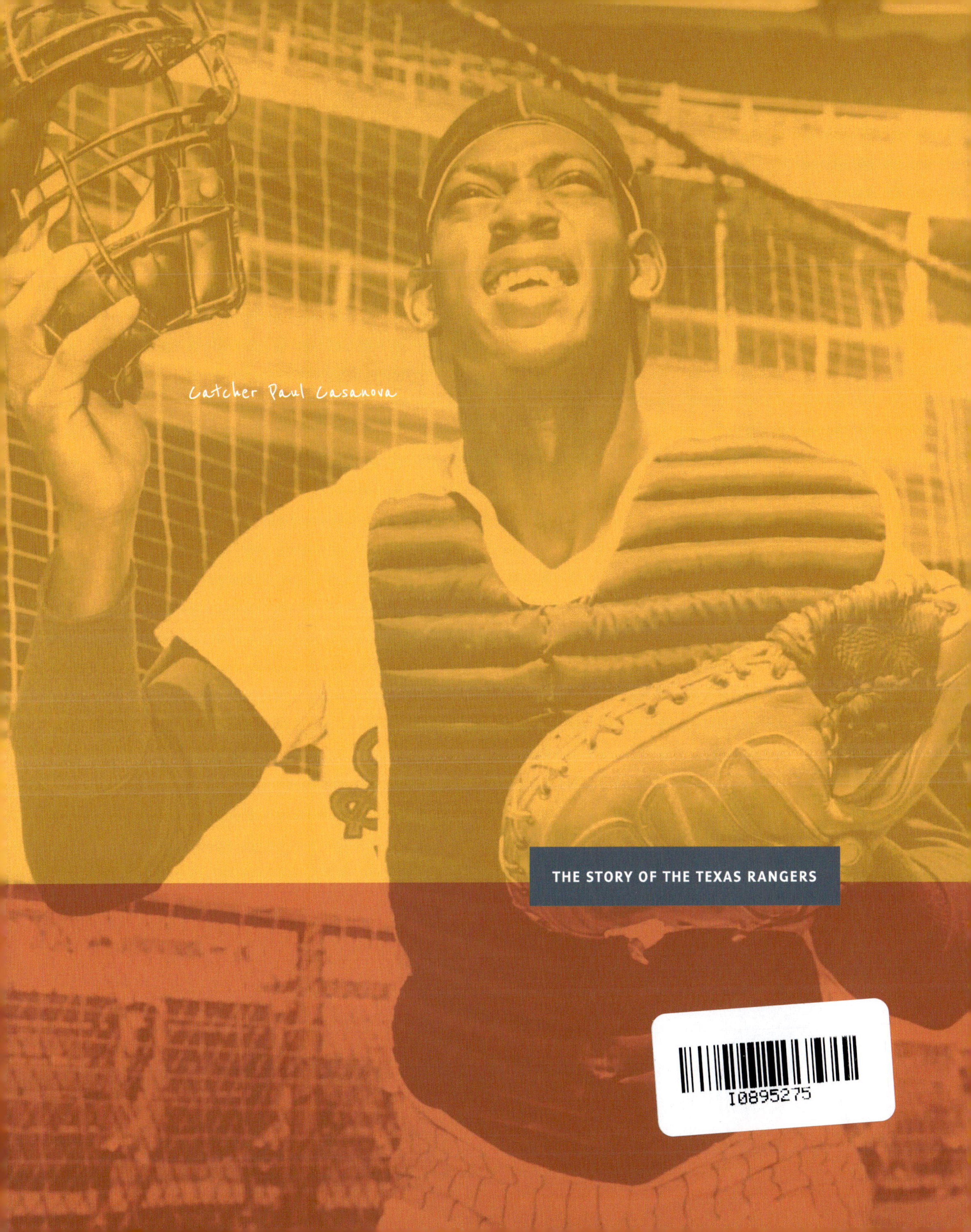

Catcher Paul Casanova

Pitcher Lance Lynn

THE STORY OF THE

TEXAS RANGERS

JIM WHITING

Catcher Iván Rodríguez

CREATIVE SPORTS

CREATIVE EDUCATION / CREATIVE PAPERBACKS

Shortstop Elvis Andrus

Published by Creative Education and Creative Paperbacks
P.O. Box 227, Mankato, Minnesota 56002
Creative Education and Creative Paperbacks are imprints of
The Creative Company
www.thecreativecompany.us

Book Design by Graham Morgan
Art direction by Blue Design (www.bluedes.com)

Images by Alamy Stock Photo/Trask Smith/UPI, 2; Associated Press/Frank Jansky/Icon Sportswire, cover; Getty Images/B Bennett, 1, Bob Levey, 26-27, Brad Mangin, 6 (bottom, right), Chris Coduto, 11, Chris Covatta, 3, Daniel Shirey, 9, David Durochik/Diamond Images, 10, Diamond Images, 12, John Williamson, 18, Jonathan Daniel, 19, 22-23, Lloyd Fox/Baltimore Sun, 20, Louis Requena, 6 (top, right), MediaNews Group/East Bay Times, 31, Nick Cammett/Diamond Images, 30, Otto Greule Jr, 6 (bottom, left), Rich Pilling, cover, 7 (top, right), 16, Richard W. Rodriguez/Fort Worth Star-Telegram, 7 (top, left), Rob Tringali, 29, Ron Jenkins/Fort Worth Star-Telegram, 4-5, 32, Ronald Martinez, 7 (bottom, left), 7 (bottom, right), Stephen Dunn, 25, Tony Tomsic, 6 (top, left); Wikimedia Commons/Mopey1988, 10, public domain, 15

Library of Congress Cataloging-in-Publication Data
Names: Whiting, Jim, 1943– author
Title: The story of the Texas Rangers / by Jim Whiting.
Description: Mankato, Minnesota : Creative Education and Creative Paperbacks, [2026] | Series: Creative sports. Major League baseball | Includes index. | Audience: Ages 8–12 | Audience: Grades 4–6 | Summary: "Discover the Texas Rangers' thrilling journey from their origins to their recent triumphs, featuring legendary players and the Major League Baseball team's most historic moments. Written for middle-grade readers. Includes table of contents, sidebars, and index"— Provided by publisher.
Identifiers: LCCN 2025013136 (print) | LCCN 2025013137 (ebook) | ISBN 9798895811115 library binding | ISBN 9798896800644 paperback | ISBN 9798895812372 ebook
Subjects: LCSH: Texas Rangers (Baseball team)—History—Juvenile literature | Baseball—Texas—History—20th century—Juvenile literature
Classification: LCC GV875.T4 W458 2026 (print) | LCC GV875.T4 (ebook) | DDC 796.357/6409764531—dc23/eng/20250530
LC record available at https://lccn.loc.gov/2025013136
LC ebook record available at https://lccn.loc.gov

Printed in the United States

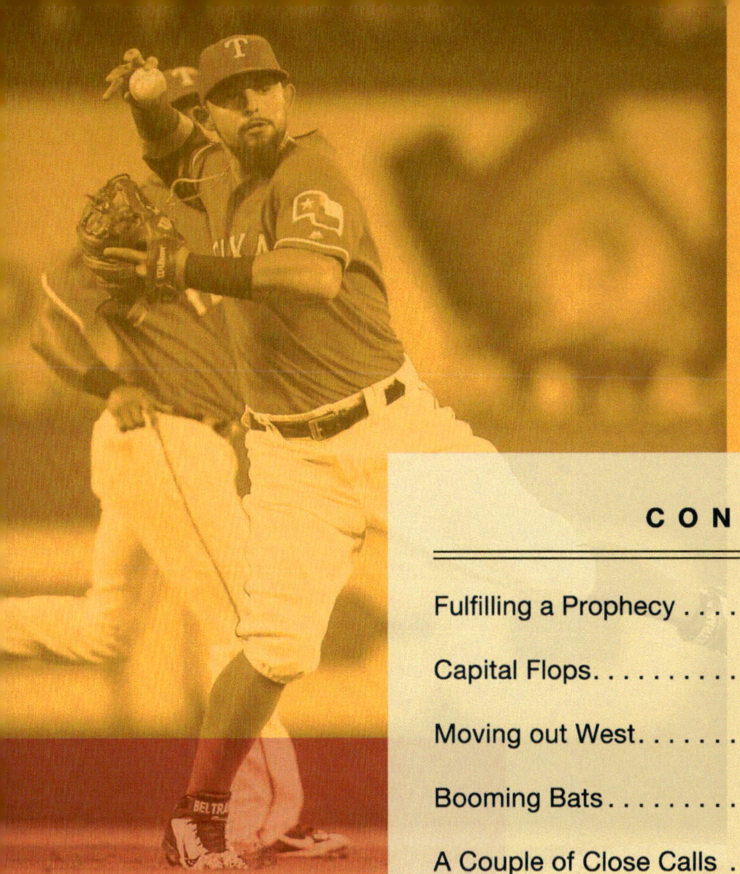

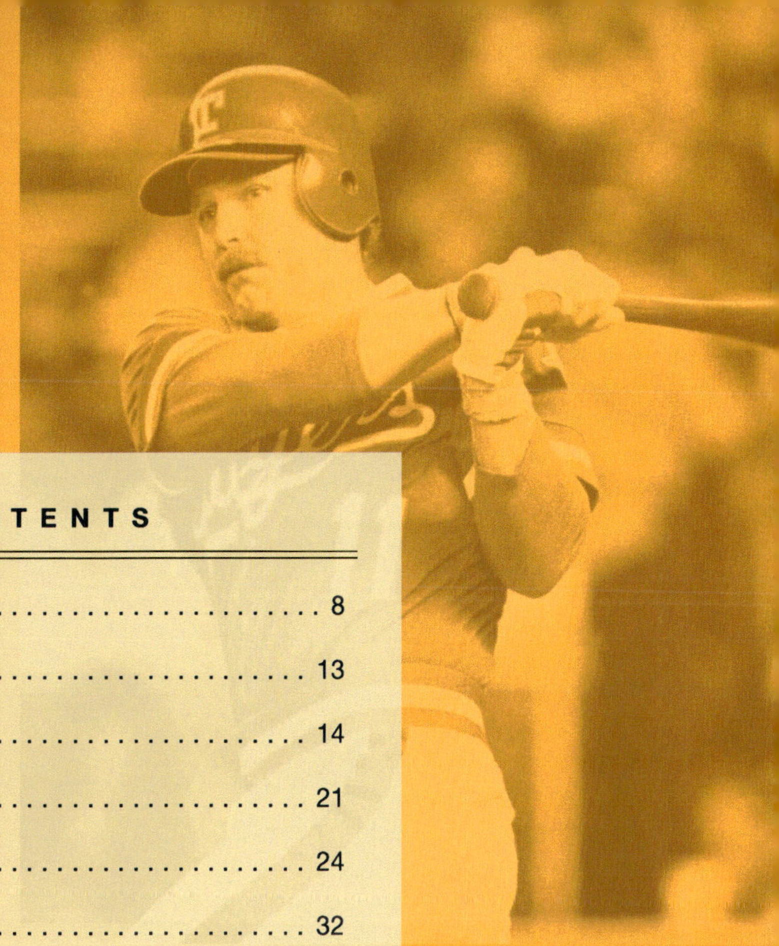

CONTENTS

EXTRA INNINGS

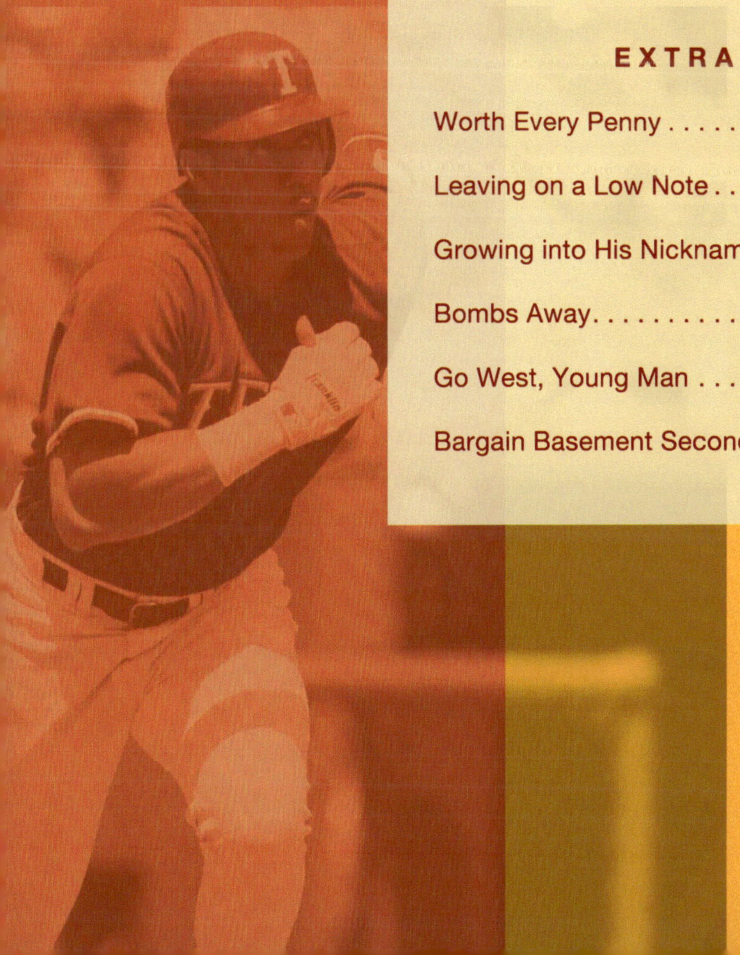

FULFILLING A PROPHECY

In 2019, the Texas Rangers of the American League (AL) West Division of Major League Baseball (MLB) had a 78–84 record. They finished a whopping 29 games behind the division-winning Houston Astros. Yet, first baseman Ronald Guzmán noted, "We don't take it as this year is over. We take it as this is the beginning of something great."

At first it seemed that Guzmán was mistaken. The team struggled in the shortened 2020 season, winning just 22 games against 38 losses. The 2021 season was even worse. The Rangers compiled a dismal 60–102 record. It was their worst record since 1973, when they won just 57 games. Things weren't much better in 2022. Their 68–94 record was 38 games behind the Astros.

Fans didn't have much optimism going into 2023, even though Texas had lured former MLB player and manager Bruce Bochy out of retirement. He previously managed the San Diego Padres and San Francisco Giants. He led the Giants to three World Series titles. "If I was going to return to managing, it had to be the right situation," Bochy said. "I strongly believe that to be the case with the Rangers, and I can't wait to get started."

The Texas Rangers celebrate after winning the 2023 World Series.

EXTRA INNINGS

COREY SEAGER
SHORTSTOP
RANGERS SEASONS: 2022–PRESENT
HEIGHT: 6-FOOT-4
WEIGHT: 215 POUNDS
KEY STATS: .280 BATTING AVERAGE, 96 HOME RUNS, 253 RBIS, 3X ALL-STAR

WORTH EVERY PENNY

The Los Angeles Dodgers made Corey Seager their top pick in the 2012 MLB Draft. He lived up to expectations. He was Rookie of the Year in 2016 and had two All-Star selections. The Rangers signed him to a 10-year, $325 million free agent contract in 2022. It was the largest contract in team history. Seager paid immediate dividends, with the first of three straight All-Star nods. His 33 home runs that season were an MLB record for a left-hand-batting shortstop. In 2023, MLB.com named him the best shortstop in baseball. He was runner-up for the AL Most Valuable Player award. "We're so grateful just to be able to watch him play every day and [for] everything that he does on a day-in and day-out basis at the plate, and the power he has," said Rangers pitcher Nathan Eovaldi.

Shortstop Corey Seager

After a 4–4 start, Texas remained above .500 for the rest of the season. Five Rangers were starters in the All-Star Game as Bochy guided the team to a 90–72 mark, which tied them with the Astros for the division title. Houston won the tiebreaker.

Texas opened postseason play by outscoring the Tampa Bay Rays 11–1 to sweep the two-game Wild Card series on the Rays' home field. The Rangers swept the 101-game-winning Baltimore Orioles in three games in the American League Division Series (ALDS).

Now they faced the Astros in the American League Championship Series (ALCS), with the winner advancing to the World Series. The Rangers won the first two games, the Astros the next three, and the Rangers took the final two by scoring a combined 20 runs. In an oddity, the visiting team won all seven games.

It was the Rangers' third appearance in the World Series, having lost in 2010 and 2011. This time they faced the Arizona Diamondbacks. Texas won Game 1, 6–5 in 11 innings. The Diamondbacks stormed back to win Game 2, 9–1. Shortstop Corey Seager's two-run home run was the difference as Texas won Game 3, 3–1. In Game 4, Texas built up an 11–1 lead after seven innings

and held on to win 11–7. The first six innings of Game 5 were scoreless as Texas remained hitless. Seager got his team's first hit in the seventh inning and scored the first run. The Rangers put the game away with four runs in the ninth inning to win 5–0. It was their first World Series title since their origin in 1961. Making the feat even more remarkable, Texas had compiled an away-game winning streak of 11 games during the playoffs.

In addition to his crucial hit in Game 5, Seager blasted three home runs. He was named the Most Valuable Player (MVP) of the Series.

And Guzmán had proven himself to be a prophet. It had taken four years, but the team had indeed achieved "something great."

CAPITAL FLOPS

For many years, MLB was a tradition in Washington, D.C. The Washington Senators were a founding member of the AL in 1901. They won the World Series in 1924. But by the late 1930s, the Senators began to decline. Attendance waned. After the 1960 season, the franchise moved to Minneapolis. There it became the Minnesota Twins.

MLB quickly decided to establish another franchise in D.C. In 1961, a new Washington Senators team began playing. It was as bad as the first one. Owner Elwood R. Quesada was displeased. "Why should I be paying guys who aren't good enough to play in the major leagues?" he asked. One of the few who was "good enough" was slugging first baseman/outfielder Frank Howard. He joined the team in 1965. Thanks to his powerful hitting, teammates called him the "Capital Punisher." Howard became a four-time All-Star. But he could not carry the whole team on his broad shoulders.

First baseman / Outfielder Frank Howard

The Senators compiled a string of losing seasons, finishing between eighth and tenth in the 10-team AL. In 1967, they rose to sixth. But even with Howard's MLB-leading 44 home runs, they tumbled back into the cellar the following season. Legendary Boston Red Sox slugger Ted Williams was hired as manager in 1969. The team posted its first winning record. It finished the season 86–76. It was a 21-game improvement over the previous season. Williams earned the AL Manager of the Year award. Pitcher Dick Bosman recorded an AL-best 2.19 earned run average (ERA). Howard hit a career-high 48 homers. He led the team with 111 runs batted in (RBIs). Senators fans began dreaming of bigger things.

Unfortunately, the team fell back under .500 in 1970. It closed 1971 with a dismal 63–93 record. Interest in the team fizzled. Attendance dwindled. Businessman Bob Short had purchased the franchise before the start of the 1969 season. He saw this loss of interest as an opportunity to head for Arlington, Texas, and take advantage of a lucrative broadcast deal. For the second time in 12 years, a D.C. baseball team was on the move.

MOVING OUT WEST

The Senators arrived in Texas in 1972 and became part of the six-team AL West Division. Short renamed the team the Texas Rangers. It honored the legendary lawmen whose legacy of protecting Texas settlers dated back to their founding in 1823 with 10 men.

The team posted an embarrassing 54–100 record in its first year in Texas. Howard was traded midseason. Williams retired. The Rangers shuffled through

EXTRA INNINGS

LEAVING ON A LOW NOTE

The Senators' final home game took place on September 30, 1971. They faced the New York Yankees. In the ninth inning, the Senators led, 7–5. But the stadium's security guards left early. More than 10,000 fans walked in without paying. They were angry that the team was relocating. The first two Yankees hitters grounded out. At that point, thinking the game was over, hundreds of fans swarmed the field. They wanted souvenirs. One grabbed first base and ran away. With security personnel gone, clearing the field was impossible. The Senators were forced to forfeit the game to New York.

EXTRA INNINGS

IVÁN RODRÍGUEZ
CATCHER
RANGERS SEASONS: 1991–2002, 2009
HEIGHT: 5-FOOT-9
WEIGHT: 205 POUNDS
KEY STATS: .304 BATTING AVERAGE, 217 HOME RUNS, 842 RBIS, 10X ALL-STAR

GROWING INTO HIS NICKNAME

Iván Rodríguez signed with the Rangers at the age of 16. He stood 5-foot-7 and weighed 165 pounds. He became known as "Pudge." He kept growing. "I'm small and strong," he explained. After his rookie season when he was just 19 years old, Rodríguez was an All-Star and Gold Glove winner for 10 years in a row. He earned the Silver Slugger award each year from 1994 through 1999. A year after becoming the youngest catcher to reach 1,000 hits, his batting average was .332 in 1999. He slammed 35 home runs and drove in 113 runs. He was voted MVP. His skill behind the plate was complemented by his powerful right arm, which routinely gunned down would-be base-stealers. Pudge entered the Baseball Hall of Fame in 2017.

three different managers in 1973. They combined to lead the team to a miserable 57–105 record.

Things improved the following season. The team won 84 games. Outfielder Jeff Burroughs hit 25 homers and batted in 118 runs. He earned the AL Most Valuable Player (MVP) award. Pitcher Ferguson Jenkins led the majors with 25 wins and 29 complete games. Jenkins said, "I didn't consider pitching to be work—I was having fun getting most hitters out in the major leagues."

For the remainder of the 1970s, the Rangers hovered near the middle of the division. The team's best performance of the decade came in 1977. It won 94 games that year. Five starters hit .284 or better. But Texas finished second.

The new decade began the same way. Third baseman Buddy Bell batted a career-high .329 in 1980. Knuckleball ace Charlie Hough arrived in July. He became a fan favorite. But the team had a bumpy ride up and down the standings. Though they ended 1981 and 1986 in second place, they never managed to top the division. At that time only the division winners advanced to the playoffs.

The franchise put together a formidable roster in 1989. Two rookies showed special promise. Third baseman Dean Palmer displayed sensational fielding. Outfielder Juan González swatted many home runs. Power hitter Rafael Palmeiro manned first base. Native Texan Nolan Ryan commanded the mound when he joined the team at the age of 42 in his 23rd MLB season. The "Ryan Express" notched 16 wins and an MLB-leading 301 strikeouts. This mix of power and pitching carried the team to an 83–79 finish. The team finished 83–79 again in 1990. But it was 20 games behind the division-leading Oakland Athletics.

Outfielder Juan González

On May 1, Ryan hurled his seventh career no-hitter, three more than any other pitcher in MLB history. At 44, he became the oldest man to throw a no-hitter. Palmeiro, Sierra, and second baseman Julio Franco all hit .307 or better. Rookie catcher Rodríguez thrilled fans with his bullet-like throws. The team put together its third straight winning season. But yet again, it remained out of the playoff picture.

The AL rearranged into three divisions in 1994. The Rangers remained in the AL West with three other teams. The shuffle marked the introduction of the Wild Card team. Unfortunately, a players' strike ended the season in August. The Rangers had been leading the division. But the playoffs were canceled. The highlight of the season came on July 28. Kenny Rogers pitched the 14th perfect game in MLB history, against the California Angels. He had been drafted in the 39th round of the 1982 MLB Draft. "It's unbelievable that I even got to the big leagues," he said. "My life would make a great movie. It has everything, mostly luck."

Pitcher Nolan Ryan

BOMBS AWAY

TEXAS RANGERS AT BALTIMORE ORIOLES

AUGUST 22, 2007

Baltimore built a 3–0 lead in the third inning of the first game of a doubleheader. In the fourth inning, Texas catcher Jarrod Saltalamacchia hit a single. It drove in two runs. Infielder Ramón Vázquez followed with a three-run homer. The batters were just getting started. The team scored 25 runs during the final four innings. Saltalamacchia and Vázquez drove in seven apiece. Texas pounded 29 hits in a 30–3 victory. It was the first time since 1897 that a team scored 30 runs. "This is something freaky," said outfielder Marlon Byrd, who hit one of the team's six home runs. "You won't see anything like this again for a long, long time." Texas won the nightcap by the more modest score of 9–7.

BOOMING BATS

Play started again in April 1995. The Rangers showcased a talented roster. Palmer posted a .336 average. Designated hitter Mickey Tettleton connected for 32 dingers. Rogers notched 17 wins. But the Rangers finished the season four and a half games shy of the playoffs.

In 1996, the Rangers finished with a 90–72 record. They finally won the AL West title, which put them in the playoffs for the first time in their history. González's 47 homers earned him MVP honors. Texas won the first game against the New York Yankees in the ALDS. But it lost the next three by a combined total of four runs and was eliminated. The team slumped back to third place in the following season.

The Rangers brought home the AL West crown in 1998 and 1999. Their bats were on fire. González slugged 45 homers in 1998. He also drove in a league-high 157 runs. He earned his second MVP award. "He is unbelievably strong and yet has such quick hands," Palmeiro said. "Even when he gets fooled [by a pitch], he can recover and then just snap his wrists—and the ball goes 450 feet." Unfortunately, the powerful Yankees swept the Rangers both times. González left town before the 2000 season. The deflated Rangers sank to the bottom of the AL West.

Texas sent shock waves through the majors before the 2001 season. It signed Seattle Mariners free-agent shortstop Álex Rodríguez to a 10-year, $252 million contract. It was the largest contract in baseball history at that time. "Our judgment is that Álex will break every record in baseball before he finishes his career," said owner Tom Hicks. "A-Rod" put his bat where his

First baseman Mark Teixeira

money was. He posted a .318 average and led the league with 52 home runs. He drove in 135 runs. But once again, the Rangers finished last. The next two seasons were nearly identical. Despite A-Rod's impressive performances, Texas remained mired in the basement.

In 2004, the Rangers traded Palmeiro. They also sent A-Rod to the Yankees. Texas received slugging second baseman Alfonso Soriano in return. His All-Star performance boosted the team to an 89–73 finish. Still, it was not enough for the playoffs.

The Rangers took third in the AL West the next two seasons. Several key players helped the team remain steady. Hank Blalock established himself as a solid third baseman. First baseman Mark Teixeira became one of baseball's biggest sluggers. He hit 43 homers and had 144 RBIs in 2005. Michael Young excelled at shortstop.

A COUPLE OF CLOSE CALLS

By 2007, the Rangers slid back into the division cellar. They surged up to second in 2008. The offense led the way. Second baseman Ian Kinsler enjoyed an All-Star season. Outfielder Josh Hamilton had a breakout season. He smacked 32 homers and led the league with 130 RBIs. Texas led the majors in many offensive categories. But it finished 21 games behind the division-leading Los Angeles Angels of Anaheim.

The Rangers posted their first winning season in five years in 2009. But they finished second. The following year made up for any lingering disappointment. Young, right fielder Nelson Cruz, and designated hitter

Outfielder Josh Hamilton

TEXAS

EXTRA INNINGS

MICHAEL YOUNG
SHORTSTOP, SECOND BASEMAN, THIRD BASEMAN
RANGERS SEASONS: 2000–12
HEIGHT: 6-FOOT-1
WEIGHT: 200 POUNDS
KEY STATS: .301 BATTING AVERAGE, 177 HOME RUNS, 984 RBIS, 7X ALL-STAR

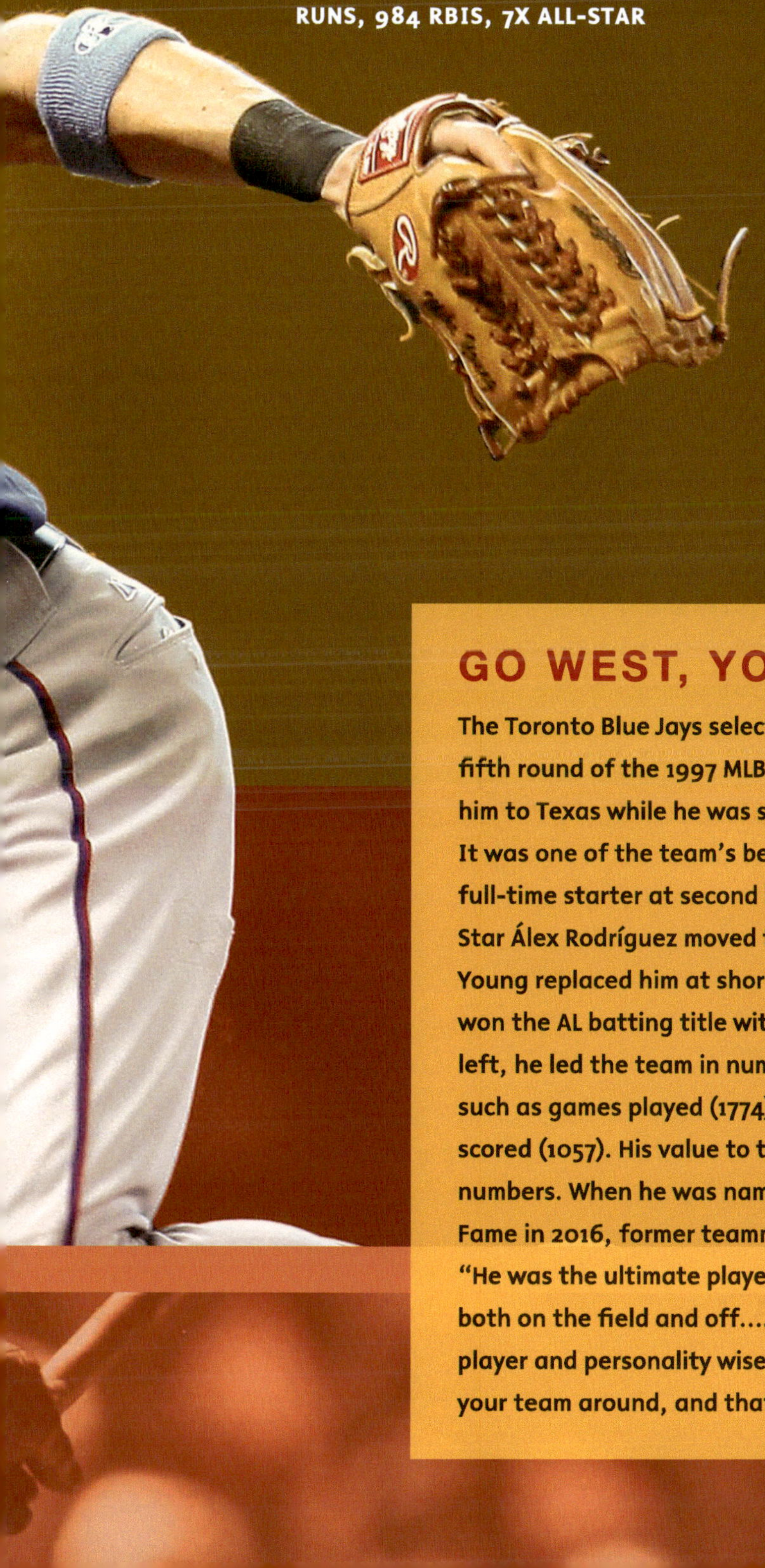

GO WEST, YOUNG MAN

The Toronto Blue Jays selected Michael Young in the fifth round of the 1997 MLB Draft, but they traded him to Texas while he was still in the minor leagues. It was one of the team's best trades. He became a full-time starter at second base in 2002. When All-Star Álex Rodríguez moved to the Yankees in 2004, Young replaced him at shortstop. The following year he won the AL batting title with a .331 average. When he left, he led the team in numerous career categories, such as games played (1774), at bats (7221), and runs scored (1057). His value to the team extended beyond numbers. When he was named to the Rangers Hall of Fame in 2016, former teammate David Murphy said, "He was the ultimate player, the ultimate team guy both on the field and off.... Michael is the type of guy, player and personality wise, that you want to build your team around, and that's what the Rangers did."

Vladimir Guerrero provided steady slugging. With 32 homers and a .359 average, Hamilton was named MVP. First-year closer Neftalí Feliz saved 40 games and won the Rookie of the Year award. The Rangers powered their way to a 90–72 record. They topped the AL West. They raced through the playoffs, toppling the Tampa Bay Rays and the Yankees. The team finally reached its first World Series. But it lost to the San Francisco Giants in five games. "We just got cold at the wrong time with the bats," said Hamilton.

The following season was even better. Texas won a franchise-record 96 games. It romped past the Rays and the Detroit Tigers in the playoffs. The Rangers faced the St. Louis Cardinals in the World Series. Texas won three of the first five games. It took a 7–5 lead into the bottom of the ninth inning of Game 6. But the Rangers could not hold on. The Cardinals won in the 11th inning to even the series. Then they cruised to a 6–2 victory in Game 7.

In 2012, the Rangers fell just short of the division title. They lost the Wild Card game to the Orioles. Texas missed the playoffs the next two seasons. Bouncing back in 2015, the Rangers captured the division title. They lost to the Toronto Blue Jays in the ALDS.

Texas improved to 95 wins in 2016. It easily topped the AL West. The Rangers again faced the Blue Jays in the ALDS. There was little suspense. Toronto opened the series with a 10–1 thrashing. The Rangers could not recover. The Blue Jays swept them in three games.

In 2017, the Rangers struggled with injuries and sub-par performances. Still, the Rangers were in contention for a Wild Card slot until late in the season. They finished 78–84. Texas dropped to 67–95 in the following season. It climbed back to 78 wins in 2019.

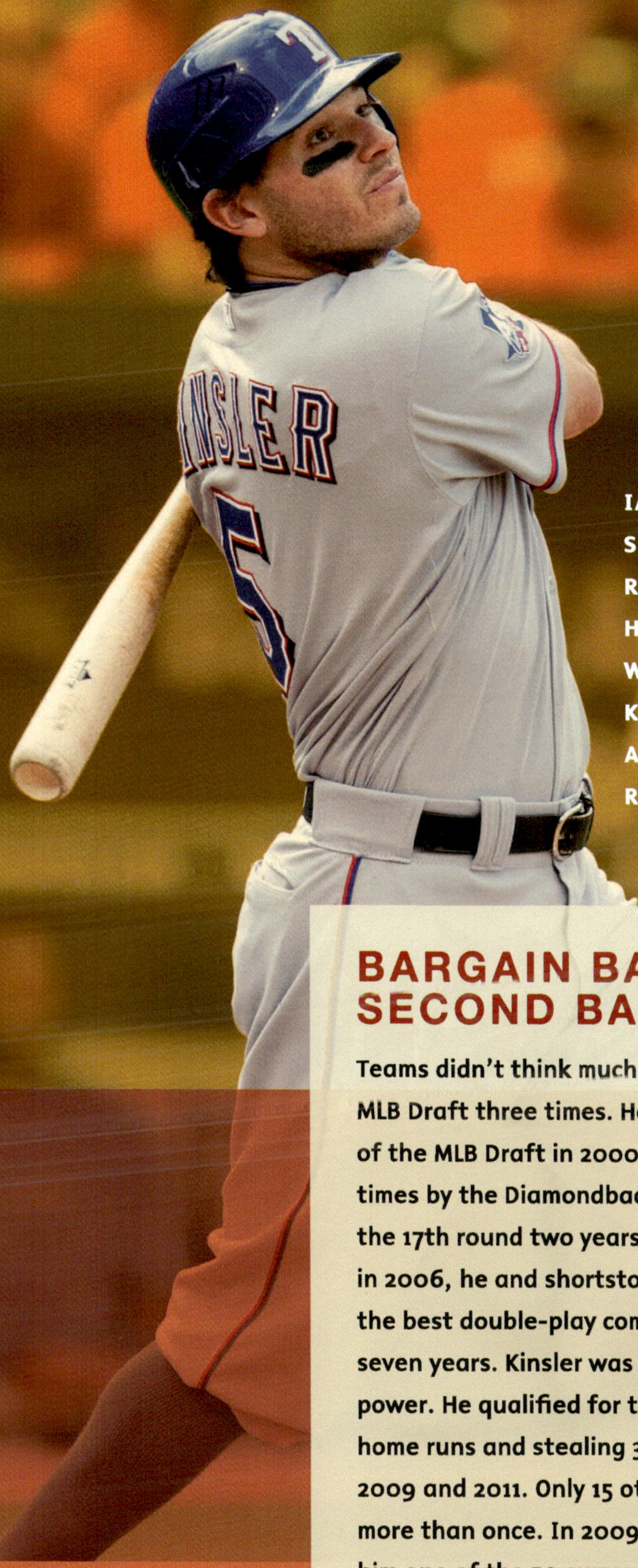

EXTRA INNINGS

IAN KINSLER
SECOND BASE
RANGERS SEASONS: 2006–13
HEIGHT: 6-FOOT-0
WEIGHT: 200 POUNDS
KEY STATS: .273 BATTING AVERAGE, 156 HOME RUNS, 539 RBIS, 3X ALL-STAR

BARGAIN BASEMENT SECOND BASEMAN

Teams didn't think much of Ian Kinsler. He entered the MLB Draft three times. He was taken in the 29th round of the MLB Draft in 2000 and 26th round in 2001, both times by the Diamondbacks. The Rangers drafted him in the 17th round two years later. When he joined the team in 2006, he and shortstop Michael Young formed one of the best double-play combinations in MLB for the next seven years. Kinsler was a combination of speed and power. He qualified for the "30-30 Club,"—hitting 30 home runs and stealing 30 bases in the same season—in 2009 and 2011. Only 15 other players have done that more than once. In 2009, The Sporting News named him one of the 50 current greatest players in baseball. Sportswriter Mike Hindman said that Kinsler was "one of the greatest 17th round picks of all time."

ENERGY TRANSFER

Catcher Jonah Heim

The COVID-19 pandemic shortened the 2020 season. Texas went just 22–38, far from playoff contention. The team struggled in the next two seasons, but it rebounded in 2023 with its World Series triumph.

Texas began the 2024 season with a 24–24 mark. But after a 1–4 road trip, they couldn't get back to the .500 level for the rest of the season. They finished with a 78–84 record.

Since moving to Texas in 1972, the Rangers have proven that they have the same grit and steely determination as their namesake Old West lawmen. They have worked hard to keep close to their competition. Although it took more than 60 years for the team to notch its first World Series title, the present-day Rangers are determined to secure another one in the near future.

Outfielder Wyatt Langford

INDEX